I WAS THERE...

The First Christmas

RAY FRANCIS and SANDY KOCH
Illustrations by Sandy Koch

I Was There ... The First Christmas

A Study Book
Copyright © 2012

ISBN: 0615585353
ISBN-13: 9780615585352

All rights reserved. No part of this work may be reproduced or transmitted in any form or by any means, electronic or mechanical, including photocopying and recording, or by any information or retrieval system, except as may be expressly permitted in the 1976 Copyright Act or in writing from the authors.

Scripture quotations in this publication are from a variety of sources, with the lead-in quotations from the Good News Translation ® (Today's English Version, Second Edition), copyright © 1992 American Bible Society, 1865, Broadway, New York, NY.

Cover art: © 2012 Sandy Koch / Alma / MI

Introduction

As Christians we consider the time of Advent to be one of the most joyous and most holy times of the year. It is a time leading up to a glorious celebration that is both spiritual and physical in nature. However, far too often we allow presents, sporting events, and so many other things to get in the way of actually appreciating the celebration leading up to the birth of the baby Jesus. The interpretive stories in this book are centered on the impending birth of Jesus, and provide you the opportunity to be involved in your own faith, and re-connect with the meaning of Advent.

Advent brings us closer to Jesus by reminding us of the fundamental principles of Hope, Peace, Joy and Love. We must consistently remind ourselves of the reason for the season to truly be engaged in the event, and focused on the *why* of Christmas. Commercialism and other non-secular activities can easily distract us from the true message. The stories in this book are all written from the unique perspectives of those who might have been alive and experiencing the time of the birth of Jesus. The thoughtful insights into the lives of people in Bethlehem, and the surrounding countryside at the time leading up to the grand event, give you the opportunity to participate in an understanding of the events of the time, and the issues surrounding ordinary people facing an extraordinary situation.

So, read the stories, read the suggested Bible verses, and engage in conversation with someone about their own perception of the stories, and the meaning of Advent. It is your faith, and your opportunity to grow closer to Jesus.

Table of Contents

Introduction i

Hope

Jonathan's Story, *Larry Ward* 1
The Angel, *Pat Evans* 7
Mara's Story, *Sandra Woodruff* 9
Study Guide 18

Peace

The Innkeeper, *Helen-Ruth Hendon* 21
Something Different, *Elizabeth Baxter* 26
The Night Jesus Was Born, *Ruthann Anderson* 29
Study Guide 32

Joy

Simeon as Witness, *Nancy Korb* 35
Tis the Reason for the Season, *Harla Gillespie* 38
The Gift of the Child, *Michelle Tyree* 39
Study Guide 42

Love

Gabriel – A Two-Part Mission, *Elizabeth Baxter* 45
Joseph's Story, *Larry Ward* 49
Elizabeth, *Elizabeth Baxter* 53
Study Guide 55

Afterward 56

Hope

Jonathan's Story

The Angel

Mara's Story

Jonathan's Story

Titus 3:7 – So that being justified by his grace we might become heirs according to the hope of eternal life.

Yes, I know Joseph. The Joseph of Nazareth who has a wife named Mary and a son named Y'shua. That is the Joseph I know. The people of this village in Galilee are close. Not on the main road to anywhere, we have bonded together as a family would. And we all have the same goal in life, to bring honor and glory to our God. Here is my version of what went on when Joseph's son Y'shua was born. A fascinating story, miraculous even. And I still find it almost unbelievable.

Joseph was a good man, a devoted Son of Israel. He needed a wife and Mary's name was suggested. She was a precious young lady, and he asked for permission to marry her. Mary's family agreed, but before they were married rumors began to circulate Nazareth. Odd stories, they told of dreams Mary had, of a vision which appeared and was a messenger from God. This messenger supposedly talked directly to her. The rumors persisted, even when Mary returned from visiting relatives in Judea. One rumor even suggested she was with child.

I did not know what to believe. All of this was surprising and so unlike anything that had ever happened in Nazareth.

To make the situation even more complicated, just before Mary and Joseph were to marry the Romans announced that the ruler wanted to count all the people. A census. And the people needed to be counted in their ancestral towns. Nazareth had only recently been resettled by inhabitants from Judea, so that meant most men would need to leave their families and head to various villages and towns quite a distance away. My own grandparents were righteous people and had wanted to bring the worship of Adoni to the north, to Galilee. They had moved and resettled here in Nazareth, wanting to see Adoni glorified here and ask for His blessing on us to live and prosper in Galilee. So now the heads of each household would go back to their origin; I would head to Anathoth, and Joseph to Bethlehem.

Another rumor surfaced, that Mary would be traveling with Joseph for the census. She was not yet his wife, so this was extremely peculiar. No other women were going with their men, as they needed to take care of the family, livestock and crops. I believed this was the way things should be done, as they had always been done. There was no way of telling how long we would all be gone.

So strange. I decided I should speak with Joseph. I wanted to know what was happening, what he was thinking. Being close as brothers, we had no secrets from each other, yet I felt he was not being open on the decisions he was making for himself and his future.

"Joseph, my brother. Peace. How are you?"

"Peace to you, Jonathan," Joseph said. "I am well."

I paused and decided to start by asking a general question. "Joseph how is Mary and how are the plans for the wedding?"

"Mary is well. And you already know the wedding has been postponed. I do not think you are seeing me today to inquire about the health of Mary or myself."

"Joseph, you are so perceptive," I replied, still unsure how to bring up this matter. "I see you are going to Bethlehem for the census, and Mary is going with you. She is still not yet your wife. Why are you letting her? Women are not needed at the census. It does not seem like a good idea to have her travel with you, particularly since you are not wed."

"Jonathan, Mary's parents have allowed me to talk with her about this. She asked me if she could go, and I see no reason not to allow it. I can use her help, and she needs me."

I was shocked to hear him speak of Mary as a help on the journey. "You need a woman's help on a journey to Bethlehem? You will be traveling with many men who can help you. She will be extra work, a burden. There must be more you are not telling me."

"Yes, there is. But first, tell me what rumors you are hearing in the village?" Joseph was very calm and quiet, choosing his words carefully.

I did not want to tell him. After all, rumors are…rumors. I did not want to embarrass him, or Mary. Yet he had asked.

"Well, the stories suggest Mary has heard voices in her dreams, and has had some sort of vision from God. And there are also tales that she is with child, but I know that cannot be true. You are a righteous man, a son of Abraham."

"Thank you, my brother." Joseph hesitated and then drew nearer.

"You have been close to me, as a brother. I will tell you what has happened and am asking you to keep what I am about to tell you to yourself. Share it with no one but our God." Joseph spoke slowly and softly.

"Yes, my brother Joseph, I can do that." Jonathan knew it would be a challenge, but he could do this for his dear friend.

"Jonathan, Mary is, indeed, with child." Joseph looked his friend directly in the eye as he solemnly spoke.

I was shocked; this news took my breath away. I could not believe this was true. How should I respond? Stammering slightly, I couldn't hold back the words.

"Then it is true. She is going to have a child. How could you do this? This is a betrayal of our customs and our laws. God is not pleased. This will ruin our village and our witness in Galilee."

"Yes, I understand your indignation. And there is more to this story." Slowly Joseph continued. "I am not the father."

I was so relieved to hear this.

"I knew a righteous man like you would not have caused this. It must have happened when Mary traveled to Judea to visit her relative, Elizabeth. That is what must have happened. Some scoundrel must have violated her. She should speak up and not let wild speculation fly about the village." Jonathan was so relieved he could hardly get the words out.

Joseph sighed heavily and continued. I will always remember his words, spoken with assurance and love.

"God, Adoni, is the father of the child."

This statement shocked me even more than the first. I felt like I was hearing riddles or a children's fable.

"What! Adoni dwells in the heavens. God has not children. He cannot father a child with a mortal woman! This sounds like a Roman or Greek story about one of their own gods." I was hurt that Joseph did not trust him enough to tell him the truth.

But amazingly, Joseph was not troubled by my outburst. I could not believe how peaceful he was in his reaction. Continuing to look straight at me, he solemnly spoke.

"Jonathan, as Adoni is my witness, this is a true story I tell you. I know she is my betrothed. I have spoken to Mary's parents, and with her, at great length. Though it sounds unbelievable, I know it to be true.

I WAS THERE…

Mary is righteous and devoted to God. I know she is young, but she would never lie to me or to anyone else. I want you to listen as I briefly tell you what has happened."

I waited for the story, knowing I needed to keep an open mind. I had come for the truth, and now I needed to hear it.

"One day when Mary was praying, an Angel of the Lord appeared to her and told her she would have a son, one who would be great among the Lord's people. He also told her this son would reign over the house of Jacob forever. The Angel said that the Spirit of God would make this happen. Following this vision, Adoni inspired Mary to compose a beautiful psalm about His love for all His people. When she first told me I did not believe her and wanted to divorce quickly. But then, and I can hardly believe this myself, I had a dream inspired by God! The same Angel spoke to me and told me the details of Mary's account were true. The Angel said I should not put her away, but should marry her as we had planned. I love her, Jonathan, and want to honor her. It is a strange story, but I believe God and I believe her. Because of this, we will go to Bethlehem together and be married there. She can give birth quietly, away from the wagging tongues of Nazareth."

I did not know what to think. This sounded so unreal, nothing I had heard of before. I did not want to hurt my dear friend's feelings, but how could I believe this story?

"Joseph, I think you must be mistaken. First, God and His holy Angels do not talk to women. Is there anywhere in the Torah or the Writings or the Scrolls that says God talks to a woman? Women don't have visions. And they do not compose psalms or songs. Joseph, women don't think, they just follow our orders."

"Jonathan, you have judged harshly a woman you barely know. I have made a commitment to her, which I will keep. Mary has made a commitment to Adoni, and I believe her." Joseph continued, resolutely. "Mary is not like other women. She does think, and wonder, and dream. She believes God can speak to women, as He does to men. She has even memorized some of the holy writings that we hear in Synagogue. I believe her. I trust her. I believe God has visited her and he has confirmed that in a dream to me. I still want her as my wife, and we will go to Bethlehem together. I don't know what will happen, but we will follow Adoni. This is for you to know, Jonathan, as I trust you like a brother. All these events will reveal themselves in time. So please keep our secrets for now, until the time is right."

"If what you say is true, when will this be? When will we all know what has been revealed to you?" Jonathan was trying to understand, and wanted something concrete to hang on to.

"I don't know. But I do know Adoni does not want this story retold quite yet. Perhaps when we return from Bethlehem, with the child, and can speak with our families rationally, then will be the time. Or perhaps the time will be revealed to us in another way. We will have to wait and see. Only Adoni knows the plan."

I was troubled by all this, but Joseph was my closest friend. How could I not trust him?

"This is a difficult request, but these are difficult times for all of us. Since I am as a brother to you, I pledge to do as you say. I will not tell anyone yet. But I still don't know if I believe all you have said. Angels speaking to women, you having a vision yourself, how does this fit into how God works in Israel? We have not seen anything like this before. I will let you go and must trust that you are making the right decision. Please travel with my blessing; Adoni's safety with you."

"I will take your blessing, and keep Adoni's safety with me." Joseph embraced me, demonstrating his love and trust.

Several years have passed, and since then Joseph has even more unusual stories to tell. Tales of events in Bethlehem and Egypt before returning home to Nazareth. They are remarkable stories of God's protection and guidance and the courage it takes to follow God's path. I still have a hard time believing them, yet the lives of Mary and Joseph are rich and strong.

And there is the boy, Y'shua. Their son is a remarkable child. Very peaceful and obedient, he is a quick learner. I think God does have His hand on him, and maybe he is marked for a special responsibility in Israel. I wonder what the Angel meant when he told Mary that he would reign over Israel forever. That is, if you can believe such a tale. And if it is true, I hope I will live long enough to see such a miracle unfold. I will wait and watch…and see.

I WAS THERE...

Matthew 1:18-21; Luke 1: 26-56

Ward Schmidt
First United Methodist Church
ww.fmhouston.com
Houston, TX
Houston Bay Area Emmaus Community

The Angel

Romans 8:24-25 – For in this hope we are saved. Now hope that is seen is not hope. For who hopes for what he sees? But if we hope for what we do not see, we wait for it with patience.

As he flew, the air was cold and crisp.
His wings beat a cadence of love and joy as if the drums of
Heaven were surrounding a call to arms.
As he glided on the wind
His heart was full and his thoughts raced ….
How could I have been the one chosen to announce His birth?
I am just a lowly warrior in an army of angels.
What was God thinking when He called out my name?
As He laid out His plan, I could scarcely breathe.
I had never even been close to the throne of glory and
There I was, standing at His feet as He spoke the name of Jesus
In hushed tones.
All I could think as my head bowed and my knees wobbled was
Why me, Lord?
He flew on.
Thoughts of love, fear, humbleness, and gratitude filled him
With such wonder that he almost passed by the field of shepherds.
Slowing to a flutter, he set gently down among the sheep.
As he lifted his wings and rose to his full height,
He could see the fear and wonder in the eyes of the shepherds.
It was the same fear and wonder that he had just experienced at the feet of
Father God.
As he spoke the words that would be repeated for generations to come,
He felt awe and wonder.
He spoke of a Savior
A King

I WAS THERE...

The Son of God
Who would one day rule in majesty and splendor over all the earth.
As he finished his assignment and lifted his wings
His heart soared with joy and he cried out
Holy, Holy, Holy is the Lord!
Today a savior is born!

Pat Evans
Abilene, TX

Mara's Story

Romans 15:13 – May the god of hope fill you with all joy and peace in believing, so that by the power of the Holy Spirit you may abound in hope.

The night is cold, the wind sharp. I feel it in my achy joints and bones. It is so cold I move a little closer to the fire, wrapping my shawl closer. My eyes grow heavy and I begin to feel myself drift back in time. I have seen and experienced many wonders in my old years. I can hear the children playing … and I laugh quietly to myself. No, not children. Grandchildren.

Please, they will beg. Tell us tales by the wayside. I will smile and begin again, the story they have heard so many times and which seems ever fresh in memory, though the events happened long before their father was born.

They settle close round my knees, feeling my touch, and warmth from the fire. As they quickly get comfortable and quiet they look up, their eyes reflecting the fire light like that bright, shimmering star of long ago.

Outside the wind picks up and begins a mournful sound. My Sara looks up expectantly at me as I begin my tale, and I am reminded that I was just her age when I met them. Time wavers from this warm, safe house of my oldest son, to that of an old, dark cave, lit by a single stub of an old candle. The gusts of wind catching the tiny flame, the dancing light highlighting the animals sheltered there to be silhouetted against the walls.

I didn't mind the wind, or the dark. My animal friends helped keep me warm, and I was safe in the recesses of the cave. No one could see me unless they knew where to look. Sometimes I would go out to the hills to watch the stars. They shimmered like a thousand Roman campfires around the village, so pretty. I had been watching one particular star since early spring. I thought of it as my star; it seemed to shine brighter every night, just for me.

I never stayed out long; I was afraid of people. I would always hide if I heard someone near. Nevertheless, I was drawn each night to watch my star, no matter how cold it got. Just seeing it made me feel warm, safe and peaceful. I watched that star, and it looked like it was getting a little bigger and brighter every night. Eventually, I would grow sleepy and return to my animal friends. My family in the cave.

Such a different family from the one of my past. I had vague memories of a mother with long dark shimmering hair, smiling eyes, a soft voice, and a loving touch. My father was also a distant memory. He was very tall, with dark hair and eyes, and a voice which commanded authority and respect. I remember his eyes the most, as he looked at my mother and me. His eyes were tender and loving; mother was the light of his world and I was part of that light. He had spent a lot of time away, as mother would tell how he owned many camels, bringing beautiful things from far away.

Once we made the trip with him. I remember the rocking of the camel mother and I rode on, and the camel bells and noises of the caravan as we moved along each day. Every day we got closer to home, mother seemed to become sicker, weak with a cough and fever. We were passing a village and father went to consult the local healer. This healer said mother could not ride on with the caravan or she might die. Father and the healer walked a little further away from our resting spot, and spoke quietly. Father was told of an inn nearby where mother could stay and perhaps get well. But it would cost him a high price. Father laughed and told the old woman that money was not a problem; he just wanted his beloved wife well.

Off to the inn they went, where father paid the innkeeper very well to care for us. Father also issued a warning that we be well taken care of well until his return…or there would be a price to pay. No one ever wanted to deal with father when he was angry. The healer was paid well and asked to do the best she could. Father departed after hugs and tears, and prayers.

Mother seemed to grow stronger for a while, and then her cough became much worse. The healer tried all she could to cure her, but mother was too weak. She seemed to fade away each day, and by late summer Mother was gone.

Father did not return that season, or the next. The innkeeper said I could earn my keep; it appeared he was too afraid of father to put me out. He said I could tend the animals and live out in the cave, telling me I was too skinny and young to be of any other value … just yet.

HOPE

The cave suited me well. I took the few goats and cows out to pasture each day, and learned to milk and make cheese. The animals became my friends and I was relatively happy. The chickens laid eggs, which I gathered, and occasionally they laid one in a different area, meant for me to find for my own use. I understood the animals better than I understood people.

I was afraid of people, their noise and rough ways. The older girls who lived in the inn made fun of me living like I did, and would sometimes throw rocks at me. It was always a relief to come back to this cave. With the animals I was safe.

The only time I was glad to be out among the people was when I would run with the other village children to greet the caravans. I was always hoping to see my father come to town with his camels and riches. But he didn't come. And after I while I stopped looking for him.

One winter the village was filled with Roman soldiers, taxmen, caravans and travelers. Caesar had decreed that all had to go to their ancestral homes to register and pay taxes. I was now a maiden, a bit taller and more rounded in shape. I stayed far away from the Roman soldiers and traders from the caravans, which was difficult to do with so much going on. The men would come to the inn to visit the women who lived and worked there. These women would laugh at me when they passed by on their afternoon walks, asking me when I was going to give up living with the animals in the stable and join them. I remember how my face turned hot with embarrassment, and how I would hurry away with the sound of their laughter ringing in my ears as they disappeared into the inn with another customer.

I learned quickly to make myself very small, smear dirt on my face, and keep my hair uncombed. I could make myself disappear into a crowd, too. However, one dark night as I was returning from my stargazing, a large, dark shadow grabbed me and I felt a sharp pain on my face as I struggled. That's all I remember until I woke much later, on the hill behind the cave. One eye was swollen shut; the other noted the passage of time according to the star movements across the heavens. I felt sore and dirty, hurting everywhere. Someone had hurt me, and I had no one to go to. Who would believe me, anyway? I could be stoned to death and no one would know the truth. Staggering home to the safety of my cave, I cleaned up as best I could. Taking an old shawl which had been a cast off gift from one of the women at the inn, I carefully covered my head and face.

The next morning I met the innkeeper and his wife as I was taking the animals out to pasture. He pulled aside the shawl and questioned me about the bruises. I told him I had fallen and hit my face … not that they believed me. They looked at each other, then at me again, deciding to question me no further. The innkeeper simply told me to stay out of the way, and out of sight.

Late that night I was conflicted about whether to go and see my star. Though I wanted to seek the comfort of that consistent and shining gift from the heavens, I didn't want to run the risk of seeing someone and getting reported to the innkeeper, or worse. Seeing my star won out, and I carefully stayed hidden from view as much as possible as I made my way out of the stable and headed toward the edge of town. The night air was cold, clean and refreshing, and my face seemed to hurt less.

Across the square, at the door to the inn, I had noticed a young couple who was being turned away by the innkeeper. Everything was so crowded with everyone in town for the census. This couple looked so weary, and as they turned away from the door I could see that the woman was heavy with child. No, not a woman. I could see by the lamp hanging at the inn's door that she was quite young, maybe just a few years older than I was. Her face, drawn with pain, broke my heart. I hurried after them, covering as much of my face as I could.

"Please, sir, please wait a moment," I called out.

"Yes, how can I help you?" The tall man stopped and smiled.

"I do not need your help, sir, but I have a warm and dry place you might share with me. It's not fancy, but it's so cold out here and I think she should be somewhere out of the night air. It's not far from here, just across the square."

The man turned and quietly spoke to his wife, who nodded. The way he looked at her reminded me of how my father looked at my mother, and a tiny tear escaped from my good eye. I quickly wiped it away with the back of my hand, as though a gust of wind had caused my eye to water. He turned the donkey around to follow me, as I lead them to the cave and showed them my sleeping quarters by the cow's manger. I had just filled it that day with fresh, sweet-smelling hay.

Helping his wife down, they smiled at me, grateful for a place to rest out of the cold night.

"Thank you. My name is Mary and this is my husband, Joseph. What is your name?" Joseph unloaded the pack and Mary sank gratefully down on a pile of hay.

"I am called Mara, after my mother." I felt shy and awkward, avoiding direct eye contact with this lovely lady.

While Joseph moved some of the hay around to make a bed for Mary, we talked a bit. Mary wanted to know why I was living here in this cave instead of being in a home with a family. I told her about the caravan and my father, and my mother's death. The innkeeper had told me I was only about 6 or 7 when I was left here, and I told Mary about his offer to have me live here and earn my keep caring for the animals.

While we were talking Mary seemed to be having a difficult time getting comfortable, and before long it was apparent she was in labor. Breathing deeply, she walked around a bit, bending to ease her burden, trying to stay calm and focused. I had seen animals deliver their babies and knew to some extent what to expect. Mary seemed so calm, though she was obviously in pain, and she occasionally smiled at Joseph as if they shared a secret.

My scarf slipped from my head as I hurried around trying to gather some clean linens and offer sips of water to Mary. She gasped in surprise and Joseph turned toward the sound. I quickly replaced the head scarf and avoided their eyes. Mary reached out her hand and pulled me close to where she had settled to rest.

"Oh, dearest one," Mary crooned as she reached up and caressed my face, gently wiping away my tears, which I'd barely noticed were falling. "Joseph, please bring me my bag. I have some salve my mother sent with me. Please give me one of the soft cloths and fresh water."

Mary really was only a few years older than I was, but it felt so good to be gently touched and cared for. Joseph's face was grim and hard, but his voice gentle as he questioned me about what had happened. Though I was afraid, I felt I could trust him with the truth. I told Mary and Joseph the whole story, including the part about my special star and how it always comforted me.

Joseph shook his head in anger, but Mary's face was sad. There was little time to linger over the details of the story, however, as Mary's labor was becoming more intense. Joseph had gone to seek help, but no one would come. As Mary settled into the rhythm of deep breaths and strong contractions, Joseph and I worked to help her deliver the child. A beautiful, pink, round baby boy. After he was cleaned and wrapped in cloth from Mary's bag, the baby was settled within her arms. She motioned me to come over and whispered his name to me … Jesus. Just the whispering of the baby's name gave me a feeling of wonder. Joseph looked all aglow, a proud father filled with wonder at this small bundle in his wife's arms.

"Jesus. That's your name, little son. Jesus." Mary said the words as if whispering a prayer, and that little baby opened his eyes and looked straight at me.

I know babies aren't supposed to see clearly right away, but he looked at me and wiggled one of his arms free of the swaddling cloth. This little babe reached up and touched my face as I bent to see him more closely. Suddenly, my face did not hurt anymore! The swelling around my eye faded and was gone! I could see clearly again. My body didn't hurt, either. The bruises were gone! A wonderful, warm and safe feeling overcame me, and I cried.

Mary gasped quietly and called Joseph over. They spoke for a few moments in hushed voices while I sat still, too amazed to move. Mary finally looked at me and spoke.

"Mara, you must keep your face covered as usual, and not tell anyone what has happened. This is God's miracle, but many will not understand. For fear of our lives, you must tell no one. Will you promise?" The conviction in her voice, and on Joseph's face, was strong, yet kind. I would keep this promise.

Later that night there were visitors, shepherds from the hills who told of angels coming to see them to tell them of a babe lying in a manger, wrapped in swaddling cloths. They had followed the star, my star, which was HIS star, guiding them to this stable. I kept myself hidden in the shadows until they left.

The next morning Joseph went to see the taxmen, and then to look for a better place to stay. He found a small house close by, and they asked me to come with them. Joseph went to the innkeeper and told him that he was taking me with him. The innkeeper laughed and told him to take me. I was good for nothing and more animal than human.

Joseph responded gruffly, "We WILL be taking her with us."

Over the next few weeks I helped Mary with the baby while Joseph did some carpentry work for the local people. One evening Mary told Joseph that God had sent me to them in their hour of need, and they couldn't leave me here. She asked Joseph to think about what should be done, and he went back to work, nodding in his quiet way.

Watching Mary, I remembered little things my mother had done. When I asked her about them and told her what I remembered, she told me that my mother must have been a good woman, teaching me with love and faith, for me to remember so much. I told Mary that I wanted to learn more, to grow into a woman such as herself, and my mother. Mary and I talked of many things, of how to be a good woman, and to love the Lord. Mary laughed and told me I was her little sea sponge, soaking up everything she told me. At night Joseph would tell me stories of the great heroes of our people.

One day Mary told me it was time for her to go to the Temple to present Jesus to the Lord, as the Law of Moses required. They made the journey and brought back many stories. While there, they met a man named Simeon and a very old woman known as Anna. They spoke in soft tones and great wonder, as they told of meeting these elders. Other members of Joseph's family were also there at the Temple, and they came to visit. Joseph and the other men talked of many things that night, including what would become of me.

The women also gathered and spoke of me, the orphan girl. Some seemed to think I should go with Mary and Joseph when they returned home to Nazareth. Others were not so sure. The question was presented to Joseph's Aunt Ruth, the oldest of those present, and considered the wisest. She told the family she would pray about this matter and see what the Lord would answer. That night, she had a dream.

When Ruth met with the family the next day, she informed them that through the dream God had given her the answer of how best to help the young Mara.

"Ebenezer, my son, agrees with me. After praying over the Lord's message to me, given through a dream, it is agreed that Mara will come with us. She will be of help to me, as well as help care for Ebenezer's motherless child."

It did not matter to them that I had lived in a cave with the animals, nor did it matter that I had no family of my own. It mattered only that Mary and Joseph loved me and thought me worthy of a family, and that the Lord had given His blessing.

This plan was laid out to me by Joseph and Mary, and they asked what I thought. This was no small decision on the part of Ruth and Ebenezer, taking in a stranger as part of the extended family. The room was very quiet, waiting for the final decision to be made, which was really extraordinary. These people really cared about what I thought. They were treating me as a respected part of their community, as an equal. How could I do anything else but accept this offer, when the Lord so smiled on all of us and on a bright future? With my shy nod of agreement the room shook with laughter and words of welcome and cheer.

None of this would have happened if it hadn't been for the birth of the baby Jesus, and my star had watched down on us all. I was truly blessed to be a part of this family, and Jesus had brought love, joy and special healing. What would our future bring? What would HIS future bring the world?

Several years later, Ebenezer asked me to be his wife. He told me that he loved me and was proud of how I had grown up a reflection of his mother. I knew I was truly blessed to be so loved by all the members of his family, and his love helped me complete my journey to wholeness.

The wind gusts grew stronger, disturbing the animals, their lowing carrying upstairs. I opened my eyes and gave a gentle sigh. All those things had happened so long ago; I smiled as I remembered my beloved husband waiting for me for our evening prayers. The loving looks he always gave me reminded me still of the looks my father gave my mother, and Joseph gave Mary. The look of love and devotion. I count my life's blessings daily.

After the children were tucked in for the night, I went to Ebenezer, and thought back to the time I saw Mary and Joseph on their return from Egypt. Mary had been eager to hear about my life with my new family and as a bride to cousin Ebenezer. I had shared a secret with Mary, one I had never shared with anyone except my husband.

"Mary, on the night Jesus was born, do you remember what happened?"

"Yes," she smiled. "I will never forget. So many things. So many blessings. I remember your kindness as you shared your shelter, and your help at the birth of my son. I also remember how he touched your face and your bruises faded at his touch. This has been a treasured secret, has it not? A secret between family members."

"Yes, Mary, all my bruises were healed at his touch. But not just the visible wounds. He healed my whole body, making me once again untouched, clean, and pure. This was made known to us on our wedding night! All from a baby's touch! His touch, which brought healing, love, and a gift of a new life." There were tears in the eyes of both women, as they embraced.

"That was only the beginning," said Mary. "Watch. One day the world will know, and be healed. Praise the Lord."

Sandra Woodruff
Bedias, TX
Bedias United Methodist Church
Matthew 2:1-24 and Luke 2:1-40

I WAS THERE...

Hope

Study Questions

Jonathan's Story
1. How could Joseph by "justified by Grace" in his situation?
2. How does Jonathan demonstrate Grace?
3. How can we demonstrate Grace in our daily lives?

The Angel
1. What would be your reaction to seeing an angel?
2. What would you think of the message just delivered to you?
3. What would you do first?

Mara's Story
1. Describe Mara's experiences with family initially, and how they informed her as she grew up.
2. What was Mara's reaction to meeting Mary and Joseph? Did she see anything special in them, or their situation?
3. What would have been your own reaction had you been faced with the same situation of seeing a homeless couple looking for a place to sleep?
4. What do Mara's actions say about Hope in her life, before she met Mary and Joseph, and after?
5. What does the baby Jesus symbolize to Mara?

How do these three stories exemplify the theme of "Hope"? How are these stories connected?

Peace

The Innkeeper

Something Different

The Night Jesus Was Born

The Innkeeper

Philippians 4:6-7 – Do not be anxious about anything, but in everything by prayer and supplication with thanksgiving let your requests be made known to God. And the peace of God, which surpasses all understanding, will guard your hearts and your minds in Christ Jesus.

I absolutely cannot believe what I've done. My business is booming, all my rooms are full, and I go and say something I already regret. What was I thinking? More importantly, what will everyone else think?

I suppose I could have turned them away, but they said they had come all the way from Nazareth. That's a four days walk. Plus, they looked so dusty and tired. If they had arrived earlier in the day I could have given them a room, but with the Imperial census the roads have been more crowded than usual with soldiers and caravans. So I was left with only two options; turn them away or offer them the stable. Some instinct told me to offer the stable, and before I even considered all the consequences, I had done just that.

Joseph, holding the reins of the donkey, said that any shelter was okay. His wife didn't speak, but she smiled sweetly when she heard my offer. So now here I am, at dusk, walking them through the dimly lit courtyard to the stable. Some of the other guests are still outside, but if they notice us at all they probably think we are going to the stable to leave the donkey.

Joseph looks like a man of much strength, but he is very gentle as he helps his wife, Mary, from the donkey. Lifting my lantern, I am alarmed to realize that she is expecting a baby, and soon! I hadn't noticed that as she sat bundled on the donkey. A cold chill runs through my body as I realize I have given them a chilly stable to stay in, which can't be very healthy for the expectant mother. Panic was setting in.

I hurriedly assist Joseph in clearing a work bench for his wife to rest on, but she said she'd rather stand and stretch for a few minutes. Mary seems very weary, so I rush back to the inn and return with a blanket for her, one I can hardly spare. I also bring an extra lantern. When I realize how crowded the stable is, I stumble about rearranging mangers, water troughs and straw so there is a small area in which they can rest. I shake my head, seriously questioning the wisdom of housing them for the night.

I WAS THERE...

With relief, I see they have traveled with a straw bag containing bread and cheese. I wish I had thought to bring some of the fig cake Martha baked today, and I make myself a promise to bring some out in the morning. After I ask Joseph if he noticed the well in the courtyard, he assures me he will fill their goatskin bag before retiring for the night.

Not knowing what else to do, I wish them a good rest and walk slowly back to the inn. Other travelers are still lingering in the courtyard, laughing and talking loudly. I approach them and speak quietly, hoping they will follow my lead. I think perhaps Joseph and Mary will be glad for the company of livestock rather than this rowdy group of travelers.

Wearily climbing the stairs to our family's quarters, I note that the children are now settled on their mats for the night. Often, when the inn has vacancies, we allow the children a room of their own, but tonight they are crowded in with Martha and me. There is only one lamp lit, and I am grateful for the thriving business that will allow Martha to purchase new sandals for the growing children, and a reserve of oil for the lamps. As I check on the children, I am stunned to realize that Leah, our oldest daughters, is about the same age as Mary.

I tried to fall asleep, hoping that I won't become the laughing stock of Bethlehem for housing guests in my stable. Maybe I'll even be lucky and find Joseph and Mary gone in the morning, and no one will ever know they were here in the first place. Just as I drift off, I hear a commotion below the open window. What on earth could that be?

I pull aside the blanket covering the window to our room. Sheep fill the courtyard. Sheep! Am I fully awake? I hurriedly throw on my mantle and slip on my sandals. Others are stirring below as I rush down the steps. As if having guests in the stable isn't enough, I now have a courtyard full of sheep! I realize that my hard-earned reputation as a good innkeeper may be in jeopardy.

There are people in the doorway of the stable. As I grow nearer I note that one of them is the shepherd Joel, and the other is his brother Jonah. They turn to me with the most unusual smiles I have ever seen on their faces. Normally timid boys, they step aside to allow me to enter the stable.

"It was the angels," said Joel. "They told us to come. They scared us half to death at first. There we were on the hillside just talking about what a clear night it was. And then there was this angel! Then a whole sky full of angels! They told us to come and see the baby. What else could we do?"

As my eyes adjust to the light of the rising sun, I am dumbfounded by what I see in the warm glow of the stable. Me, the wily barterer in the village. Me, the teller of long stories to my guests around a courtyard fire. In this moment I can find no words to express my wonder. I sense others enter behind me. Martha gasps and hurries to Mary's side. She quietly talks to her as our Leah, John, and Andrew crowd around. Silence falls as all look to the manger.

There lies a baby, swaddled tightly and looking up at his mother. He is resting in the manger of straw as if it were a down-filled mattress. Joseph is close enough to keep a hand protectively on Mary's back as he smiles at the baby, and then at all who are here to witness this event. His gaze finally rests on my face, and in his look is gratitude. Without this stable they may have been forced to find a cave in the hillside, with no extra blankets, lantern or fresh water. Joseph also knows my reputation might be on the line, but he is glad to have had this accommodation.

As a few of the inn guests curiously approach, the animals begin to stir. There is already noise outside the stable with the flock of lambs filling the courtyard. I ask my children and the shepherds to step outside with me. I consider asking the inn guests to leave the young family alone, but I realize that I have just witnessed something beautiful, and holy. What other explanation could there be, if angels really told the shepherds to come and witness the birth? How can I deny others a peek inside? Especially as Joseph and Mary seemed to welcome the attention their son was receiving.

I find Joel and Jonah speaking softly to their sheep as they lead them from the courtyard. They excitedly repeat the story of angels appearing in the heavens over the hillside. Jonah tells me that the angels sang "Gloria" so loudly that he thought the whole town, the whole valley, also heard the message! They say that the angels told them that this baby would be their Savior. Their Messiah! The young men seem bewildered, but joyful. I know these boys and their father, and certainly nothing in their past causes me to suspect that they were drinking too much wine last night, or that they are lying to me now.

"We must go tell our family and friends so they can come and see the baby, too!" Joel began to gather his flock together.

I walk slowly back to the stable. Things are calmer now, as some of the guests have removed their animals on departure. Martha has sent Leah to our room for clean blankets and some of the fig cake. She wants to move the young family into our quarters, but they refuse and assure us that they are comfortable here with the animals. Martha has so much compassion that she looks to me to argue with Joseph, but I can see that his mind is made up. I assure him that as soon as we have an empty guest room I will move them to better lodgings. Joseph nods, and Mary also agrees with her smile.

Unable to resist any longer, I approach the manger. The precious baby boy yawns and appears to be falling asleep amid all the chaos around him. His face glows in the soft morning light. I cautiously reach out a hand and touch the top of his tiny head. My fingers relax there, and I lay my whole palm on his head. I feel a strange and wonderful peace. I've never before felt anything like this. I am so still that my breathing seems to almost stop. Even more strangely, I am embarrassed to realize that there are tears in my eyes. Looking quickly at Mary and Joseph to see if they've noticed, they smile knowingly at me. I am mesmerized, unable to leave the baby's side, and I fall to my knees beside the manger.

I don't know how long I stayed that way, but a quiet serenity has settled inside the stable. There is peace such as I have never experienced before. Lingering, just watching the baby and listening to his quiet breathing, even the chores pulling at my conscience cannot force me to leave this little one's side. Not just yet.

Finally, knowing that Mary and Joseph need privacy and rest, I rise to leave.

"I hope your stay here will be a long one, for I would like to hear your story. Where you are from, who your families are, your profession, and your plans for your newborn son are all things I would like to hear about at length. Does he have a name?"

"Yes," Mary replied. "It is Jesus."

Walking away from the stable I realize that I find the shepherd's story of the angels visit quite believable. I am no longer tired, and the song in my heart leads me to whistle softly. I even chuckle at the mess left in my courtyard by our visiting flock of sheep. And I am finally not concerned in the least what people will say about this young couple having a child in my stable. How could I have doubted for a moment the instinct to reach out a helping hand to these people, unconventional as it might have been? Why all the worry?

Though confused and awed by the events of the past few hours, I know in my heart that I have been privileged to be a part of something unforgettable, something historic, an event of immeasurable importance. Maybe I will be honored to be remembered as part of this story of a beautiful baby boy named Jesus, born in my inn's stable on a starry night when angels sang to shepherds on a hillside. Maybe the shepherds and angels will tell others about the baby, as well. Maybe he truly is the promised Messiah. Glory to God!

Helen-Ruth Hendon
First United Methodist Church
Canton, MS
Luke 2:7

I WAS THERE...

Something Different

Matthew 5:9 – Blessed are the peacemakers, for they shall be called sons of God.

It was several months ago when I first felt it. I woke up one morning and sensed something was different. I glanced about me, but everything was as I had left it when I lay down the night before. As I went about my chores throughout the day I watched, but I could not discern any difference from any other day. Maybe the sun seemed to shine a little brighter, but that must simply be my imagination, an indication that I was in a good mood.

The next day was much the same, awaking with the same feeling of expectation but finding nothing different. And the next day was more of the same. The feeling stayed with me for weeks, at times keeping me up at night, wondering why I was feeling so much anticipation. Then, one starry night, all was made clear.

I had been allowed to accompany my younger brother into the fields to deliver food to our other brothers who were tending the sheep. We arrived late, after a late start, but for some inexplicable reason I was excited. I love my brothers, but I had never experienced such a sense of anticipation at seeing them. It had to be something else. My brothers, however, were less than excited, for their flocks seemed restless and would not settle down to sleep. It was as if they, too, were excited. Something was going to happen; the air itself seemed electric.

For a moment fear filled my heart. What was this feeling? My brothers assumed a storm was coming, or some other danger, but the sky was crystal clear. I had never seen stars shine so brightly; they seemed to light up the night, particularly over Bethlehem. Surely such a beautiful night would only bring blessing, not danger.

Suddenly, I was aware that my brothers were watching me. I left my musings and smiled, remarking on the beautiful night.

"True," replied Gideon. "It is beautiful. But something has these animals all riled up. I just wish I knew what it was …maybe we should check the perimeter for predators one more time."

"All right, I'll do it." No one else had spoken up, so Gideon knew he'd be on his own. He stood and grabbed his staff, stalking off.

PEACE

Suddenly, a brilliant light shone around us and Gideon tripped over a stone, tumbling to the ground. We all froze, terrified, for before us stood a figure fearsome in beauty and glory. My heart pounding in my ears, I wondered what this vision meant! Was this it? Were we now going to die?

The angel spoke, "Do not be afraid...."

And I knew there was nothing to fear.

"I bring you good news of great joy that will be for all people."

I caught my breath. This was it! All the anticipation I'd been feeling, the excitement of the past few days. It was before me right now, and all creation seemed to be waiting for the next words he spoke.

"Today, in the town of David, a Savior has been born to you; he is Christ the Lord. This will be a sign to you: You will find a baby wrapped in cloths and lying in a manger."

Then, in an instant, before the words even passed from our ears to our brains, the sky split open with an even more luminous light, as an army of angels filled the air, with beauty almost too much to bear. They raised shiny swords and their voices swelled,

"Glory to God in the highest and on earth peace to men on whom his favor rests."

At first I thought it was a mighty battle cry, yet it was the most beautiful thing I had ever heard, striking fear and awe and joy all at once. Even now I am not certain whether the mighty host sang or whether their cry only awakened a song within me. I only know that it was perfect in every way. The wind seemed to join in and the birds as well. The trees raised their branches, and the sheep danced. It was a taste of heaven that I will never forget.

And then they were gone. The joy lingered over the stillness. No one moved, not even the sheep; we all could have been statues we were so overcome by what we had witnessed.

All the earth seemed to breathe again, and we all spoke at once. Stopping, then starting; laughing, dancing and leaping as if we would never stop.

"Wait!" shouted Levi. "Why are we dancing here? Let us go see this thing that has happened!"

"Of course!"

"We must!" My brothers shouted at once, and took off running toward Bethlehem.

Only Reuben paused, asking, "What about the sheep?"

I stared at him in disbelief, shook my head, and grabbed his hand. He followed my eyes as they swept across the sky, once again filled only with stars. With one last look back, he nodded and ran with me. Our feet seemed to fly over the ground; the wind chased us on our way.

When we reached our destination we found a baby lying in a manger just as the angels had proclaimed. As I looked into his little face I felt such a peace as I had never felt before. This was what I had been waiting for, what my people had been waiting for for generations, what creation itself had been longing for. As I looked at the expressions on my brother's faces I knew they felt it, too. God had not forgotten us but had broken through time to send us a Savior.

Elizabeth Baxter
Church of God
Anderson, IN

PEACE

The Night Jesus Was Born

2 Corinthians 13:11 – Finally, brothers, rejoice. Aim for restoration, comfort one another, agree with one another, live in peace; and the God of love and peace will be with you.

I will never forget the night Jesus was born. I was there and witnessed the incredible event. In those days Caesar Augustus issued a decree that a census should be taken of the entire Roman world. And everyone went to his own town to register. So Joseph had to leave the town of Nazareth in Galilee to return to Judea, to Bethlehem. He went there to register with Mary, who was pledged to be married to him, and was expecting a child.

I had the honor of carrying Mary on my back; I am a donkey named Star. We traveled a great distance on that holiest of all nights. Tired, hungry, thirsty and covered with dust, and my feet hurt. I could tell that Mary was becoming increasingly more uncomfortable the further we journeyed, as well. Mary and Joseph hoped for a good night's sleep when we reached our destination; I wished for the same.

While we were in Bethlehem Mary's time came for her baby to be born, and she gave birth to her firstborn son. She wrapped him in cloths and placed him in a manger in the stable, because there was no room for them in the inn. The stable was a fine place for a donkey like me, but Mary, Joseph and their baby deserved something better, in my opinion. But they didn't seem to mind. That little baby they called Jesus was such a good baby. He seemed to take everything in stride and rarely cried. I have a feeling he would have been content under any circumstances.

I actually liked being in the stable, as I'd missed the companionship of other animals during our journey. However, there were a few problems having humans in this environment. Bossy Bessie kept mooing orders to the rest of us. I wonder who left *her* in charge! And she was cranky! Bessie and her big mouth made a huge racket. All the while Little Lamb was frolicking about, stirring up dust. Sometimes he even playfully kicked the straw around. Handsome Horse continued eating his hay, undaunted by the happenings around him. All this activity would surely cause Mary, Joseph and the baby some anxiety so I tried to smooth things out.

"Friends, let's try to be very quiet and not cause any disturbances."

Bossy quickly chimed in, "What difference does it make? If I want to moo, I'll moo!"

"It does make a difference; there is a newborn in our presence. From my experience, babies need extra sleep, and they can sleep better if it is quiet. And Mary is exhausted after giving birth, and Joseph is tired from walking for miles during our journey. I am also so tired that I can barely stay awake and would love some sleep. Please try to be considerate of others."

"I guess I can be quiet for a *little* while, if I must."

"Thank you, Bessie."

"Little Lamb, maybe you could be a little less effervescent and not bleat quite so much?" I asked.

"But I have lots of energy and am having fun! Look how high I can jump. What if I get dust up my nose and have to sneeze? Will that make too much noise, too?" Little Lamb seemed a bit whiny.

"Of course you may sneeze if you have the need, but would you please try to mellow a little and control the rest of your actions for the sake of others? Maybe you can save your jumping until after Mary, Joseph and Baby Jesus leave."

"Okay, I'll try. I am beginning to feel a little sleepy, anyway."

Eventually, Bossie Bessie stopped mooing orders gruffly and Little Lamb drifted off to sleep. Peace and quiet were restored in the stable.

God did not give us brains that work like those of humans, but He gave us other qualities, such as compassion. We pay close attention to our surroundings because our lives depend on it. We watch carefully and listen to everything. How many humans do you know who do that? We are experts at reading body language and are so observant that not a single twitch in a muscle can remain undetected. We knew how special Baby Jesus was by the conversations we heard and from the actions we observed by those present.

We sensed that this was a very special night for humankind. The tiny infant in the manger was more than he at first appeared to be. We heard the shepherds who came discussing a vision they had seen. An angel of the Lord appeared to them, and the glory of the Lord shone around them, and they were terrified. But the angel said to them:

"Do not be afraid. I bring you good news of great joy that will be for all people. Today in the town of David a Savior has been born to you; he is Christ the Lord. This will be a sign to you: You will find a baby wrapped in cloths and lying in a manger."

We wonder, the other animals and I, if humans know how fortunate they are. God gave them the greatest gift of all with the birth of Jesus that night – the opportunity for eternal life. Are humans willing to work for life eternal with God the Father in Heaven? They only have to believe and follow the word of God.

Take it from those of us who witnessed what happened in that stable that night that Jesus was born. We saw and heard first hand. Believe. Follow the word of God. You will be saved.

Luke 2

Ruthann P. Anderson
Willow Oak Christian Church
www.willowoakchristianchurch.com

Peace
Study Questions

The Innkeeper
1. How peaceful was the life of the innkeeper before meeting Mary and Joseph?
2. How did the events of the birth affect the innkeeper?
3. How did the experience of peace change for the innkeeper after the birth? How will it affect his life?

Something Different
1. What was the feeling that the young lady was experiencing at the beginning of the story? How was that feeling developed through the story?
2. Did the brothers in the story experience peaceful life? What leads you to this conclusion?
3. Why did they follow the star?
4. Describe the change which settled in over the brothers, following the heavenly visit.

The Night Jesus Was Born
1. How does the donkey describe the journey to Bethlehem?
2. What was Mary and Joseph's reaction to sharing the stable with the animals? What makes you think this?
3. How did the animals experience peace through the birth?

How do these three stories exemplify the theme of "Peace"? How are they connected?

Joy

Simeon as Witness

Tis the Reason for the Season

The Gift of the Child

Simeon as Witness

Psalms 96: 11-13 – Let the heavens be glad, and let the earth rejoice; let the sea roar, and all that fills it; let the field exult, and everything in it! Then shall all the trees of the forest sing for joy before the LORD, for he comes to judge the earth. He will judge the world in righteousness and the people in his faithfulness.

My name is Simeon and I am but a lowly Jewish priest, elder and translator. I have lived many years, and seen many things. However, two things stand out to me. The first is that long ago I read in the scrolls called Isaiah that the Christ would come from a virgin. I thought, "How can this be?" Oh, how I doubted. How could I have been so unbelieving? Do I not serve the ONE True God? For a long time I puzzled over this. And one evening, while I was walking by my favorite stream, enjoying the breeze that comes with the night, I was overcome by something I saw. Fear came upon me as I realized I was looking into the face of an angel.

As I gazed into the angel's face I did not see condemnation. I saw acceptance, joy, and excitement. It was then that I heard this glorious being actually speak to me! I was awed, and wondered why I was given this privilege of privileges. I listened carefully and was overcome with the message I was given:

"You will not die until you behold the babe who before time is the Creator and God of all!"

I thought about this statement as well as the passage in Isaiah for years to come. I continued my work as a translator, translating works from Hebrew into Greek. My favorite was to translate the Jewish scriptures for my brethren. Our native tongue is no longer being used thanks to Diaspora, the dispersion of the Jewish people from their native land of Palestine.

Besides my work as a translator, I also continued my priestly duties. I was constantly going to Jerusalem to work, shop, and perform services in the temple. Because I am always meditating on my God, I could not help but think upon what the angel told me years before. I remember being told that I would not die until I saw the Christ, the one that was to be the consolation of Israel. Oh how I long for that day! I long

I WAS THERE...

for the savior to come and save His people from all the suffering we have gone through for centuries. I look around me at the dust on the roads, and the hot sun beating down on our faces as both my people and I trudge through our day. Daily I wonder when this prophecy will be fulfilled. I get discouraged and feel like it will never happen. Yet, I remember that night long ago, and the angel. I won't doubt! I know it happened, and I know the prophecy will come true. I look up into the sky tonight and see the stars and whisper to my God, "When?" I sheepishly remind Him that I'm getting older, but He knows that so I just smile and keep waiting for my miracle.

Daily I see women bringing their babies to the temple that they may dedicate their first born to the Lord. That is our custom since Moses. I walked and kept my mind on my God. Like so many other times I thought back to that night I saw the angel, and what was told to me. This day felt different, though. Today, as I pondered these thoughts, my heart leaped! It was as if God Himself said to me:

"Today you will see the Messiah. Today you will see ME."

Today? Could it be true?

"But God, how will I know?" I looked to the heavens as I said this out loud.

It was at this moment that I turned my gaze eastward. There, in front of my eyes, was a couple coming my way. I knew who they were. Joseph, a well-respected person in our community, and a carpenter by trade, was coming out of the temple with his wife Mary, and their baby. I'd talked with them in the past. I knew the rumors that she was pregnant before the wedding. I also knew her, and knew she was upright in heart. I knew these rumors could not be true. They came to the temple quite often to pray, but it was different today. It was as if I saw a glow, like a halo around them. It was at that moment that God nudged me, and I knew.

This baby Mary held in her arms was Him...this was the promised Messiah! A miracle! He was of God! Now I understood what Isaiah had written. The Christ would come from a virgin! There He was, in her arms. Oh how my heart and soul jumped as they came toward me! I reached out and held this perfect boy, the Christ Child. I was humbled to even think that I, poor Simeon, was able to behold this Savior of the world in my arms. I was also fearful of holding him the Master, in my arms.

I can only think of two things. The first is a prayer:

"Glory to Thee, O Lord, Who has revealed to those in darkness the light that knows no evening!"

The second is:

"Lord, now lettest though Thy servant depart in peace, according to Thy word. For mine eyes have seen Thy salvation this day."

Truly this was the sweetest day of my life.

Mrs. Nancy Korb
St. Andrew's Greek Orthodox Church
Lubbock, TX

I WAS THERE...

Tis the Reason for the Season

Psalms 47:1 – Clap your hands, all peoples! Shout to God with loud songs of joy!

Each Christmas season is a special one. The season of Advent brings its teachings of love, hope, joy and peace. It's not about the lights, Christmas trees, glitter or buying of gifts for everyone. The teaching brings forth a joy, one I have grown to experience more fully over time.

In 2006 I attended an Emmaus walk at the beautiful lake shore of Flathead Lake. It was an experience that forever changed my life. When the Lord called my husband to attend his own Emmaus walk two years later we then had the opportunity to share a special insight into who we were in God's eyes. We both grew in our service and spiritual lives through the year and became closer in our faith to the Lord.

Advent that year was even more meaningful. The message of the season grew in strength as Christmas approached. We experienced a new feeling of the wonder of His birth. Though we hadn't planned to attend Christmas Eve services due to inclement weather, distance to travel, and preparing dinner for twelve the next day, when the phone rang, our plans changed.

It was Pastor Bob. He asked if we would like to usher and light the candles for the candle-light service. Of course we said yes, and were so glad we did. The candles reflected a special closeness of God to us all, no words necessary. It was special for us to assist the Lord in his message. I think of Mary and Joseph in a stable and the birthing of a child and how they must have felt. God promised them a great gift of his Son.

We also need to carry that great promise within us this year of our Lord, with celebration in our lives. Give thanks every day of our lives to our Creator.

Harla Gillespie
Toston, MT

The Gift of the Child

Isaiah 12:6 - ...Shout, and sing for joy, O inhabitant of Zion, for great in your midst is the Holy One of Israel.

The closer Joachim was to his home, the slower his pace became. He had endured months of doubt, and months of neighbors scorn. He knew he could live according to Moses' Law, and only prayed the recent uproar would die away. But if his daughter and her new husband were seen at his house, he knew the controversy would start anew.

As he remembered his recent visitor, his chest felt tight and it felt like a large rock was slowly sinking into the pit of his stomach. The visitor had been traveling from Bethlehem and stopped at Joachim's house to give warm greetings and blessings. He had wished to meet the father of Mary. At that moment, Joachim knew word was traveling at the rate of a raging wildfire. Wouldn't this ever die away?

The sun was beginning to fade. The air was crisp, and a light wind blew against Joachim's weathered face. The beautiful day seemed sacrilege to Joachim's mood. It was a perfect day for a journey, and perhaps this would be the day his daughter arrived with her new husband.

Joachim arrived at his home and was surprisingly disappointed to find no guests. The house was filled with an array of welcoming scents. The heated wax of the candle intermingled with the clean scent of the newly swept earth floor. The heady yeast of the freshly baked bread tantalized Joachim's nose as he crossed the threshold. Anna's voice rose over the scents:

> *Praise the Lord, O my soul;*
> *All my inmost being, praise His holy name.*
> *Praise the Lord, O my soul,*
> *And forget not all His benefits-*
> *For who forgives all your sins*
> *And heals all your diseases;*
> *Who redeems your life from the pit*
> *And crowns you with love and*
> *Compassion;*
> *Who satisfies your desires with good things*
> *So that your youth is renewed like the*
> *Eagles?*

I WAS THERE…

Joachim began washing for the evening meal. While washing, he watched Anna's hands scrub the table. Her hands were graceful, deceivingly fragile in appearance. The palms were white, fleshy, yet curiously well worn. If you looked carefully, calluses studded fingertips and the bottom pads of each finger. These were the small, strong hands of his beloved wife.

She looked up and met Joachim's eyes. Her eyes were dancing with excitement.

"Blessed is our God, who saved us from slavery. He has brought forth the Messiah, who will be in our very house."

"Such blasphemy! It will not be spoken in my house!" The force of his fierce whisper clearly shocked Anna. He turned from her and strode across the room. As he began to cross the threshold, he was met by his stoic son-in-law.

Embarrassed to be found in such a state, Joachim quickly fought back his anger.

"Joseph, welcome."

Hearing Joseph's name, Anna rushed to the door in greeting.

"Joseph! I hope your journey was well."

"Thank you." Stepping aside, Joseph turned to allow Mary to enter, carrying the small bundle of controversy.

Joachim, Anna and Joseph stood in the house, watching Mary cross the threshold with the babe. The air was heavy in anticipation. Mary raised her brows and stared into her father's eyes. No shame, apologies, or silent plea for forgiveness were present. Her gaze was steady, sure and confident. Joachim's eyes fell to the swaddled infant in her arms.

"This is the babe? He looks quite ordinary." Joachim's eyes were not mocking; his open face showed only surprise. "This is our Messiah?"

"Yes, Abba. He is our Savior." Mary smiled at her father. Never had she spoken with such authority, or with such grace. She held the baby towards Joachim.

Joachim's eyes widened. His breath was coming in short bursts. His arms began to reach for the child as Jesus' eyes opened. The babe's warm eyes gazed upon his grandfather with such serenity and love that Joachim caught his breath.

Joachim's face broke into a smile. His entire being felt new. A sense of peace swept through the room. Joachim's arms enveloped the baby, as he was enveloped in joy. The babe snuggled against Joachim's chest and resumed his slumber. It was such a simple gesture, yet so profound in the promise.

Searching his wife's face, he saw her cheeks were wet with tears of joy.

"Welcome into my heart, my beautiful Savior." Joachim whispered. "And welcome to the world You have come to save."

Michelle Tyree
Amarillo, TX
First Baptist Church of Amarillo

I WAS THERE…

Joy
Study Guide

Simeon as Witness
1. How did the experience with the angel change Simeon?
2. How would you feel if the same news were given to you? How would it change your life?
3. Describe the joy Simeon felt at the birth of the baby Jesus. When he saw Him for the first time.
4. How did seeing Mary and Joseph at the Temple change his life?

Tis the Reason for the Season
1. How do we, as Christians, celebrate things with joy?
2. What are the things that should bring us joy?
3. How can we move to focus on faith-based, rather than physically-based things to bring us joy?

The Gift of the Child
1. How were the individuals in the story reacting to the arrival of the baby in the house?
2. What joy did the baby bring to Joachim and Anna? How did their joy influence Mary's parents?
3. How long would their joy last? What is the lesson of this gift?

How do these three stories exemplify the theme of "Joy"? How are these stories connected?

Love

Gabriel – a Two-Part Mission

Joseph's Story

Elizabeth

LOVE

Gabriel – A Two-Part Mission

Song of Solomon 8:6-7 – Set me as a seal upon your heart, as a seal upon your arm, for love is strong as death; jealousy is fierce as the grave. Its flashes are flashes of fire, the very flame of the LORD. Many waters cannot quench love, neither can floods drown it. If a man offered for love all the wealth of his house, he would be utterly despised.

God called me to his throne room for a special mission. As He laid out his plan for me, my head spun a bit with the details. God's love for the humans had called him to extreme measures to restore them to Him. I knew something would have to be done in order that they could join us here, but I could never have imagined the lengths God would go to. I have loved watching him weave this beautiful love story from the very beginning, in the garden, through deserts and wilderness and grand temples, but I could not have predicted this twist in the tale.

God explained to me that he would send his son to earth, to show his precious creation the width, height, breadth, and depth of his love. Granted, this was not such a shocker, for even I could foresee that He would have to get involved, but the form Jesus would take totally blew my mind. Jesus, the glory of heaven, the joy and light of heaven, would be leaving us and going to earth as a baby. A baby! It seemed a great risk to me, but I knew the Father would be looking over him. How amazing for Jesus to fit, to become a human being with all the power and glory of God completely contained in a fragile, weak form! Though I have been witness to many amazing things, there was nothing that could compare to this plan.

Preparations had to be made for such a wondrous thing to happen, and that's where I came in. Another human, a very special person, was to prepare the way for Jesus, and he would also begin as an infant. The birth of this child would also be miraculous and I dressed as befitted the occasion.

In the Holy of Holies I was to meet a priest, one who was devout and humble. He would probably be ready to accept a heavenly vision, as he embraced his faith whole-heartedly. However, I was very wrong.

Zechariah, the recipient of the great message from God, was not prepared for my visit. In fact, I nearly scared him out of his wits! I was

I WAS THERE...

in a place God's presence was expected to dwell, but clearly this was too much for him.

I quickly reassured him that he had nothing to fear (unless you consider such a tremendous responsibility as raising the one who would go before the Lord as frightening). Zechariah became calm enough to focus on what I was telling him. He and his wife, though both past the age of childbearing, were going to have a son, one who was going to prepare the world for its Savior, and they would have to raise him differently than a typical Jewish boy. God was at last going to rescue his people and use Zechariah and his wife in the plan!

I thought I had covered all my bases, but poor Zechariah just stared at me.

"How can I be sure of this?" he asked.

This man wanted proof! An angel of the Lord had just appeared to him in the most sacred place in the temple and given an amazing message, but the man did not believe it right away – he questioned God's miracle, wanting more proof!

I was disappointed by his doubt of God's power and grace, so I informed him exactly who I was, one who stood in the presence of the most high God. I also informed Zechariah that there was a penalty for doubting this message. From this moment forward, until the birth of the babe, he would not be able to speak. There would be no telling the good news, no sharing with others the blessings bestowed upon him and his family.

And it was so. Zechariah opened his mouth to speak and no words came forth. He used his facial expressions and gestures to show his remorse, and his awareness of the great gift and honor he was being given, but was not able to make a sound. The awe and joy I observed are what I will always remember, as well as the horror of what was happening due to his doubt. It was too bad he came to this realization so late, as it would have made his explanations to everyone so much easier.

Upon my return I was prepared for my next mission. This one would be just as difficult to explain to the recipients, and even more powerful a message. I must deliver a message to the one who would carry the God of heaven in her womb, and raise him as her own, to be the Savior of the world. This time I would not be appearing to a priest in a hallowed section of the temple. I would appear to a young girl, one who was not even allowed in the majority of the temple, in a small town far from Jerusalem. I would appear on an ordinary day and deliver a message which would change the course of history. Who could tell how this would go?

I found the girl alone in her home, having just returned from an errand. Taking a deep breath, I made myself visible. She merely stared at me, as if she saw angels every day! A bit surprised by her lack of reaction, I introduced myself.

"Greetings, you who are highly favored! The Lord is with you."

This young girl appeared troubled, but not afraid as most humans are. Who was this girl, who appeared unfazed by a visit from an angel?

"What does this mean?" she asked me.

On familiar ground now, I assured her she had nothing to fear. With great pleasure I delivered the good news.

"You have found favor with God, and been chosen to bear the Son of God. Salvation is coming at last!"

She listened humbly and processed the words for a few minutes in silence. I took the time to look at this chosen one. Obviously not from great wealth or position, betrothed to a carpenter, she would be raising this Son of God in a world of hard work. One young lady, humble and steadfast, would raise the child of God. She looked at me again, biting her lip slightly.

"How can this be…since I am a virgin?"

This was a truly remarkable young woman, one who asked how this miracle would take place, not asking to have this message proven, not dismissing this message as impossible. She believed. She knew.

"The Holy Spirit will come upon you, and the power of the Most High will overshadow you. Your cousin has also been chosen to be part of God's grace; though barren, she will also conceive a child with her husband who will help bring God's human presence to light. Clearly, nothing is impossible with God's power and grace." I was so excited to be explaining this gift to a young lady so ready to take on the responsibility asked of her.

"I am the Lord's servant," responded this child. "May it be to me as you have said."

I WAS THERE...

The greatest message ever delivered to humanity, and this girl, this child had agreed to it as if she had just been asked to pray daily. Leaving her to ponder this miracle, I couldn't wait to tell the others about my mission. How would this story play out? Time would tell.

Elizabeth Baxter
Church of God
Anderson, IN

LOVE

Joseph's Story

Philippians 2:2 – Complete my joy by being of the same mind, having the same love, being in full accord and of one mind.

You must know how exited I was when Mary consented to be my wife! Me, a poor carpenter, living in the tiny hamlet of Nazareth. What a prospect for a happy life together with the girl of my dreams!

I had known this beautiful girl most of my life. Our families were respected members of our little Jewish community. Ordinary people, trying to eke out a living in the northern part of Israel, and peace-loving, we always tried to do the right thing - be respectful of the Roman occupants of our country, pay our taxes as required by the government, attend synagogue, and worship, honor and adore the Lord our God of Israel. As children, Mary and I attended our small synagogue together, and enjoyed pleasant encounters at parties, bar mitzvahs, bat mitzvahs and the like.

Heli, Mary's father, and I had spoken on many occasions. As I became more interested in Mary as a possible wife, I found myself trying to impress him with my work ethic, and lead him to think of me as the time of consent came closer. One day, as I was busy building a small table for him, Heli approached me himself.

"Hello, Joseph. How is the table coming along?" Heli asked.

"I'm about finished. I should be able to deliver it the day before the next Sabbath," I responded.

"Good, good," mumbled Heli. "Joseph, I have something very important to ask you. I don't know how to ask this any other way. It's about Mary. She has reached the age of matrimony and I would consider it a blessing if you would give thought to becoming her husband. What are your feelings about this?"

"Well, I have thought about getting married, and I, well, I was wondering if you have talked to Mary about this. What does she think about marrying an ordinary carpenter?"

"Mary is willing, Joseph. I've talked to her at some length about her future. You know, she's only thirteen, but I know she would be a good wife for you. Her mother has taught her how to run a household. She's a good cook. She can sew and keep a clean house. Mary was actually elated when her mother and I talked about you as a possible husband for her. I really think this would be a perfect match for our little Mary, Joseph. I think you would be a good husband, kind and hard working."

I was thrilled beyond measure. Me, a simple carpenter, the husband of his beautiful earthly angel. So pure and innocent, was Mary. The answer to my prayers. I was absolutely giddy at the prospect of spending my life with one so precious.

Not wanting to appear too emotional about this exciting news, I simply responded that I would certainly give consideration to this proposal. I'm sure her father could see the elation in my countenance. I mean, how can you put on a dour expression when you've just been handed the best news you could ever imagine?

I actually floated across the yard between my shop and house. I could not eat the evening meal, in my excitement. Sleep came in bits and pieces, but at one point during my fitful sleep that night I dreamed about my precious Mary. Questions, so many questions. Can I support her? Will I be worthy of her? Can I be the man she will be proud of? What about children? Who would they favor? Could I possibly have a son who would follow in my footsteps, as a carpenter? It is certainly an honorable profession. I would be able to teach him my trade and skill. Together we could make a good business. Just think…a sign above our shop: *Joseph and Son, Master Carpenters*. That would make his mother proud!

I could hardly wait until morning, when I could inform Heli that I would be honored to have Mary as my wife. Little did I realize that I would soon be tested with news that would bring serious doubts about Mary. News of impropriety on Mary's part, which would challenge our cultural belief about marrying someone who was less than pure and devout.

Mary had consented to be my wife, and soon we were officially betrothed. The announcement was made, the congratulations received, and the date was set. But shortly thereafter, rumors surfaced which started to cast doubts on Mary's character, and behavior. Could it be that she was unfaithful to me? Being betrothed was tantamount to being man and wife, but she actually began to show evidence to the contrary.

If it were true, who could this man be? He had violated my intended, and if I could get my hands on him it would take a Roman Centurion to separate us. I was distraught, chagrined, and heartbroken. My first inclination was to back out of the arrangement in order to save face. In the Torah, our Holy book, Deuteronomy clearly gave us permission to write a bill of divorcement if we had any reason to believe that a wife didn't meet our standards for an honorable relationship.

Handing over a bill of divorcement might be a little premature, but on the other hand certainly something was wrong. Maybe I should get out while there was still time. Though difficult to walk away from the woman I loved, I honored God's laws so much that it seemed like the only solution.

Before doing anything official, I decided to talk with Mary and her parents about the evidence which was mounting against her. Upon arriving at their home, however, I was told that Mary had traveled to a town in Judah, somewhere in the hill country. Her cousin Elizabeth was expecting a child and she wanted to give her some company during her confinement. I had thought Elizabeth much too old for a child, but maybe that's why it was good Mary was with her.

Which left me with way too much time on my hands to worry about what to do. I certainly didn't want to disgrace Mary. I wanted to take care of this business as quietly and quickly as possible. There didn't seem any other explanation for the fact that she seemed to be with child, and that someone in the village had taken advantage of her. I refused to believe the rumors that she was a woman of loose moral fiber. When I was faced with the truth, however, I was stunned.

One night I went to bed, confusion still gripping my heart. I had a dream. Believing, as most in our culture, that dreams were a message from God, I embraced the miracle I saw before me. An angel from God appeared.

"Joseph, son of David. Don't worry about these rumors about Mary. God knows the truth and He wanted me to silence your fears. Mary is truly pregnant, but this babe she carries is Spirit conceived. God's Holy Spirit created this being."

My heart was beating so fast my bed was shaking. Completely soaked with sweat from the intensity of this vision, I listened as the angel further explained the miracle.

"Mary will bring a son into the world, but not an ordinary son, Joseph. You must understand this. When the child is born you will name him Jesus. You, as his earthly father."

I WAS THERE…

Jesus - the name which means God Saves.

"He will save His people from their sins," the angel continued. "This event is a fulfillment of the prophet who said, 'Look for this: A virgin will become pregnant and bear a son. They will name him Immanuel, which means God is with us.'"

I awoke with a start, in a state of shock. I had just experienced a close encounter with one of God's angels! I decided to do exactly what I had been commanded to do in the dream. I determined to marry her, giving her my love, devotion and support through the remainder of her pregnancy and for as long as we both lived.

Upon Mary's return from Elizabeth's, we went ahead with our plans. When it was time for the Roman census, and we were required to return to our birth place, Mary traveled with me to Bethlehem. Here she gave birth to the babe, and I named him Jesus, as I was instructed. I vowed to be the best father I could possibly be to the Son of the Most High.

And that is my story. We raised this awesome gift from God, and I did train him the skills of carpentry. We started our own business in Nazareth, a business which proved to be quite successful. And one day we built that sign to hang above the entrance to our shop: *Joseph and Son – Master Carpenters*.

I loved him dearly. And so did the world.

The Book of Matthew
Larry Ward
Pearland, TX

Elizabeth

Proverbs 10:12 – Hatred stirs up strife, but love covers all offenses.

Ah, he kicked again! What a wonderful feeling! In all my life I never thought I would experience anything as wonderful as this little life growing inside of me! For years I had endured the shame and disgrace of my barrenness. For years I had borne the suspicious glances, and ignored the whispers of the sins I must be, despite my being faithful daily to my Lord. Oh, there were times when even I began to wonder if there was some secret sin that I just could not bring myself to confess even to my own conscience. I'd lay awake hours recounting everything I had done in a day, the thoughts that had run through my mind, the feelings I had toward others, and the words I had spoken, but could not put my finger on it. I know I am not perfect, but I am fully devoted to serving my Lord and strive every day to be faithful. Yet, I remained barren. Oh, such an ugly word!

Zechariah and I had prayed and prayed for a child, and I know he had his doubts about his own faithfulness. We'd often seek each other's wisdom to see if something we had done would be considered a great enough sin to result in the shame we faced. But in those quiet times, the Lord would whisper encouragement and comfort to us and a peace would settle over us. In those times, we knew that we were not to blame and that somehow our shame would work into his greater plan.

And now it has! Even as I feel this child roll over in my womb, I cannot believe it is true! I will never forget the day Zechariah returned from his service at the temple, glowing with the news. I could tell something wonderful had happened from the moment I saw him, even though it took me hours to understand the whole story. Using hand gestures and motions he awkwardly told the story of the angel's visit, and how his doubting had caused this inability to speak. The doubting that we could be so blessed. The glow on his face told me that our prayers all these years were going to be answered, though I scarce believe it even now.

The day came when I could confirm it in my own body. I remember going to tell Zechariah and seeing the tears in his eyes. He wanted to be sure I was feeling all right, and then we sat for a long time, saying nothing, holding hands and reveling in God's goodness. We prayed to

God for this gift, and for the health of the child. Every now and then Zechariah would reach over and gently touch my stomach, as if it held the most precious jewel in the world, then he would smile and kiss my forehead.

The first day I felt him move and kick and roll over…the day we told the rest of our household and saw the shock, and joy, on their faces… every day has been a celebration. He is to be named John. I understand that the angel was very specific on that point, and how could we name him anything else? John – God has shown favor. How fitting a name is that? Exactly what his life will mean to us, as well as to everyone else whose path he crosses. He is destined for greatness, our John, as is foretold in the rest of the definition of his name.

Not only has God shown favor, he is calling our son to pave the way for an even greater gift, the Savior! After centuries of silence, the time has come and our son will be an integral part of the plan. I can hardly grasp the wonder I physically feel inside me, so wrapping my mind around what is to come is even more difficult to process.

And our role in this miracle from God? My own cousin is to be the mother of the Son of God! I knew it even before she told me; as soon as she stepped into our home and called out, John leapt inside me and God revealed the truth to me. She was carrying the Savior, my Savior, our Savior, and the Savior of the world! Oh, I could shout from the mountaintops!

Indeed, I do sing everyday now, for I cannot stop the song swelling inside me. It seems to grow, as John grows, ever larger, ever stronger. I am going to meet the Savior, the Son of God in flesh! I will be able to see him and touch him. I may not live to see the salvation he will bring, but I will live everyday for the rest of my life celebrating what is to come. And I will be able to do so with my own son by my side. A son who has his own role in the drama yet to come. God has truly shown favor.

Hallelujah! Praise the Lord!

Elizabeth Baxter
Church of God
Anderson, IN

Love
Study Questions

Gabriel

1. How did the action of sharing God's Son on earth show love?
2. How did Mary's action show unconditional love?
3. How did the love Mary showed grow?

Joseph's Story

1. How did Joseph show love in this situation?
2. Why was Joseph's show of love important for the birth of the baby?
3. How did Joseph show baby Jesus love as he grew?

Elizabeth

1. What was Elizabeth connecting to her past barrenness?
2. What is the connection between John and Jesus?
3. How is Elizabeth experiencing and sharing love?

How do these three stories exemplify the theme of "Love"? How are these stories connected?

Afterward

The "I Was There…." series of books and study guides is an on-going project. We are always on the lookout for authors willing to contribute their works. You might consider submitting a story for consideration for one of our upcoming projects:

I Was There . . . .
When Moses Came Down from The Mount.

I Was There . . .
When Jesus Rode Into Town

Non-secular titles include:

I Was There . . .
When the Chicago World's Fair Came to Town

I Was There . . .
When Man First Walked on the Moon

If you would like to submit a story for inclusion in one of these future works, please contact us at: rfrancis.skoch@gmail.com.

Best Regards — *Ray and Sandy*

www.ingramcontent.com/pod-product-compliance
Lightning Source LLC
Chambersburg PA
CBHW041307110426
42743CB00037B/20